NO-BAKE RECIPES FOR KIDS

© Copyright
All Rights Reserved, Debbie Madson, Madson Web Publishing, LLC
www.kids-cooking-activities.com

Sign up here for a free thank you gift:
http://www.kids-cooking-activities.com/kids-cooking-activities-newsletter.html

All rights Reserved. No part of this publication or the information in it may be quoted from or reproduced in any form by means such as printing, scanning, photocopying or otherwise without prior written permission of the copyright holder.

Disclaimer and Terms of Use: Effort has been made to ensure that the information in this book is accurate and complete, however, the author and the publisher do not warrant the accuracy of the information, text and graphics contained within the book due to the rapidly changing nature of science, research, known and unknown facts and internet. The Author and the publisher do not hold any responsibility for errors, omissions, or contrary interpretation of the subject matter herein. This book is presented solely for motivational and informational purposes only.

Table of Contents

Introduction 5
EATING HEALTHY 8
   Fruits 8
   Vegetables 8
   Grains 9
   Protein Foods 9
   Dairy 9
KITCHEN SAFETY RULES FOR KIDS WHO COOK
.... 11
NO BAKE BREAKFAST RECIPES 13
   Microwave Eggs 14
   Tutti-Frutti Muesli 15
   Breakfast Pinwheels 16
   Blackberry-Mango Breakfast Shake 17
   Breakfast Parfait 18
   Kicked-Up Quesadilla 19
   Wheat Waffles 20
   Morning Milkshake 21
   Breakfast Crostini 22
   Egg Tortilla Wrap 23
NO BAKE LIGHT MEAL RECIPES 24
   Cheesy chicken and veggie noodles 25
   Veggie Pita 26

- Grapefruit Salad 27
- Creamy Grape Salad 28
- Eat-the-Bowl Dip 29
- Soft Chicken Tacos 30
- Easy Arugula Salad 31
- Kid Friendly Pasta Salad 32
- Quick Tuna Patties 33
- Simple Vegetable Sushi Rolls 34
- Microwave Baked Potatoes 36
- Ham and Pickle Rollups 37
- Tortilla Sandwich Rolls 38
- Egg Salad Celery Bites Recipe 39

NO BAKE SNACK RECIPES 40
- Slam Dunk Fruit 41
- Pick-Me-Up Popcorn 42
- Banana Wands 43
- Peanut Butter-Banana Spirals 44
- Cinnamon Toast 45
- Sunshine Juice 46
- Raspberry Cream Cheese Spread 47
- Cantaloupe Melon and Berry Smoothie 48
- Fruity Fun Bars 49
- No-Bake Cinnamon Rolls 50

NO BAKE DESSERT RECIPES 51

Frozen Fruit Bites 52

Oatmeal No Bake Cookies 53

No Bake Butterscotch Oatmeal Cookies 54

No Bake Peanut Butter Cookies 55

Lemon No Bake Cheesecake 56

Chocolate Chow Mein Noodle Cookies 57

No Bake Chocolate Almond Coconut Bites 58

Chocolate-Dipped Strawberries 59

Mini Pumpkin Tarts 60

Easy Strawberry Mousse 61

Chocolate Peanut Butter Bars 62

Cranberry Ice-Cream Pie 63

Cookie Dough Bites 64

Surprise Pie 65

Easy Fudge Recipe 66

Honey Milk Balls 67

Introduction

Welcome to one of our cookbooks in our " Cooking with Kids Series"

If you have visited my website before http://www.kids-cooking-activities.com you'll know I'm a big believer in teaching kids to cook. Our slogan is **helping kids learn and grow up in the kitchen** and that is just what I'm hoping this series will interest you and your kids in doing.

Kids that learn to cook and help in the kitchen are more likely to eat what they had a hand in creating. Which means that they will be interested in trying new foods and it is a perfect opportunity to teach them new healthier options.

You can involve your kids in cooking no matter the age. We have ideas on age-appropriate tasks on our site here:

http://www.kids-cooking-activities.com/kids-cooking-lessons.html

Some tips in cooking with your kids:

- Read the recipes, ingredient lists and cooking process fully before starting
- Set out all the cooking tools
- Start with a clean workspace and stove
- Always use fresh ingredients
- Always wash your hands before cooking
- What takes an adult a short amount of time may take your child longer so be prepared

Remember to supervise your kids while they are cooking in the kitchen.

Kids gain a lot from cooking –reading skills, math, science, small motor skills, patience, and confidence achieved from accomplishing a task. This No-bake Cookbook for Kids is a nice choice for kids under ten already interested in cooking. The 50 recipes that don't require an oven or a stovetop; this enables the kids to do most of the work alone –under the supervision of an adult, of course. It's a starter cookbook for picky eaters and no other cookbook will encourage them to try out new foods with such enthusiasm. All the 50 recipes are straightforward, and each has at least a fun step a kid can perform. You'll also like the fact that the cookbook is packed with plenty of healthy dishes from breakfast to desserts and snacks. With recipes such as breakfast parfait, Kicked-up quesadilla, mini pumpkin tarts, Cranberry Ice-Cream Pie, and Tuna patties with sweet chili mayo. Yum!

WARNING: Children, please ALWAYS have someone older around when you are using a blender, food processor, knives or handling hot stuffs.

EATING HEALTHY

Whether you're a toddler or a teen, it's good to take good care of your body to stay healthy and feel happy. Eating a balanced diet is one of the best ways to do this. Eating a balanced diet means that your meals contain the recommended content of the main food groups – fruits, grains, proteins, and dairy.

Fruits

This group comprises a wide variety of fresh fruits as well as fruit products, including, canned, frozen dried fruits, and 100% fruit juice. Melons and berries, which seem to be particularly rich in nutrients, are highlighted among the most essential subcategories of this food group. While nutritionists and doctors recommend filling about half of each meal serving with vegetables and fruits, the fruit amount you should eat every day depends on your activity level, age, and gender. Kids between 2 and 6 years should get 2 servings of fruit while older kids, over age 6 years, should get 2-4 servings from the fruit group each day.

Vegetables

The vegetable group encompasses a wide range of fresh vegetables as well as vegetable products, including dried vegetables, canned vegetables, 100% vegetable juice, and frozen vegetables. The main vegetable group is divided into groups, including starchy vegetables, orange and red vegetables, dark green vegetables, other vegetables, peas, and beans. Kids between age 2 and 6 are encouraged to take 3 servings of vegetables while older kids, over age 6 years should get 3-5 servings from the vegetable group each day.

Grains

This food group is made up of two subgroups: refined grains and whole grains. Refined grains and refined grain products include traditional pasta, grits, corn flakes, and crackers. Whole grains as well as whole grain products, including oats, quinoa, whole-wheat pasta, muesli, and brown rice, tend to have a significantly higher protein and fiber level than the refined grain products. However, the majority of the refined grain products have been enriched with iron and vitamin B. Nutritionists recommend that more than half of the grain's kids eat should come from the whole-grain group.

Protein Foods

The protein food group is made up of beans, peas, soy products, seeds, nuts, eggs, seafood, fish, poultry, and meat. Although they are part of the vegetable group because of their nutrient profile and fiber content, peas, and beans are also good sources of vegetable protein. Nutritionists recommend that kids should choose lean meat and poultry and consume a wide variety of protein products to improve the overall nutritional value of their diet. For non-vegetarian kids, at least 5 ounces of protein they consume each week ought to come from seafood.

Dairy

This group mostly comprises of dairy food products that are calcium-dense. All liquid milk, most cheese and all yogurt types fall in this food group, as are calcium-rich milk-based snacks and desserts like pudding and ice cream. Nutritionists recommend kids to consume fat-free or low-fat dairy products to limit their intake of saturated fat. Kids should consume 1-2 cups of dairy foods each day.

KITCHEN SAFETY RULES FOR KIDS WHO COOK

1. Read through the whole recipe before starting. This will help you to know how long it will take and the ingredients and equipment required to make the recipe.
2. Wear an apron and tie your hair back. It is important to keep your clothes from getting dirty and the hair out of food.
3. Avoid spreading germs –wash and dry your hands well before you start and wash often as you cook. You must wash hands after handling raw poultry and meat as they may contain germs that could make you sick. You must also keep cutting boards and other utensils that touch raw poultry and meat separate from other foods for the same reason.
4. Assemble all the ingredients out on the table before you start. Grate, shred, and chop ingredients, and measure them into bowls. It makes the cooking process a lot easier!
5. Follow recipe steps exactly. If the recipe requires that milk be chilled, it must be cold.
6. Avoid putting hot things directly onto the work surface. Always use a sturdy wooden board, mat, or a trivet.
7. Wash all the fruits and vegetables before cooking or eating.
8. Always check the "used-by" and "best before" dates on all ingredients. Avoid using out-of-date foods.
9. If you cannot reach the countertop, use a wooden step or sturdy stool to help.

10. Get help! Even if you have cooked before and you know a lot about cooking, please have an adult nearby to help.
11. Close all the drawers and cabinet doors to avoid bumping into them.
12. Wipe up any spills. Wet spots can be slippery.
13. Pick up knives by their handle and avoid pointing them at anyone. ALWAYS use a knife when an adult is around and with permission.
14. Keep electric cords away from the sink, oven, and stove top.
15. Never put any sharp object such as a knife in a sink full of water. Someone could reach in the water and get hurt.
16. Don't put water on a cooking fire; use flour or baking soda to put the fire out and call for an adult to help.
17. Always use clean plates; avoid putting cooked food on a dirty or unwashed plate.
18. Don't add water to a pan with hot oil –it could splatter and burn you or anyone around.
19. Keep pot holders, dish towels, and paper towels away from the stove to avoid them catching fire.

NO BAKE BREAKFAST RECIPES

Reorganize your morning routine and keep your children well-fed by teaching them how to prepare their own breakfast. Besides being kid-friendly and easy to make, these breakfast recipes are healthy and hearty enough for every family member to enjoy.

Microwave Eggs
Ingredients
1-2 eggs per person
microwave safe bowl or mug
shredded cheese, chopped ham, or other toppings you'd like on your eggs
Salt and pepper

Directions
Using a microwave safe bowl or mug, crack 1 or 2 eggs in your bowl. Place in the microwave and cook 1 minute. Using pot holders, remove from microwave. Sprinkle with cheese, chopped ham and/or vegetables such as chopped spinach, chopped tomatoes or chopped broccoli.
Place back in microwave and cook until egg is set about 30 seconds or less.
Serve with toast and fruit.

Tutti-Frutti Muesli

Muesli mixed with fruit packs and yogurt in the nutrition and satisfies the kids all morning long.

Serving: 1
Total Time: 10 min
Ingredients
1/4 cup(s) muesli, unsweetened
1/4 cup(s) banana, diced
1 tsp. pure honey
1/4 cup(s) apple, diced
1/2 cup(s) blueberries, frozen (thawed) or fresh
1/2 cup(s) plain yogurt, low-fat or nonfat

Directions
In a bowl, stir together muesli, banana, apple, blueberries, yogurt, honey to taste.

Breakfast Pinwheels

Ham, cream cheese, tortillas, and jam are daily ingredients that your kids can transform into quick breakfast dishes.

Serving: 4
Ingredients
Baby spinach leaves
4 thinly sliced pieces of ham or turkey
4 tbsp. strawberry jam or preserves
4 to 6 ounces whipped cream cheese
4 whole grain tortillas

Directions
Set all the ingredients out on a clean surface. Teach the kids how to lay the tortillas flat.
Spread cream cheese over the tortillas; spread a layer of jam over the cheese, leaving a border all around the edges. Top with turkey or ham pieces and baby spinach leaves.
Roll them up and serve.

Blackberry-Mango Breakfast Shake

This recipe provides a great way to get more fiber and protein past pickier kids.

Serving: 4
Ingredients
3 tbsp. honey
1 cup orange juice
1 cup low-fat tofu
1 cup frozen mango slices
1 1/2 cups frozen blackberries

Directions
Blend all the ingredients in a blender until smooth. Serve immediately.
~If your kids don't like tofu, you can leave that out or replace with plain yogurt if desired.

Breakfast Parfait

Some vitamin-rich fruit and a little low-fat dairy and your kids have just started their day right, nutritionally speaking.

Serving: 1
Total Time: 10 min
Ingredients
2 tsp. wheat germ
1 cup cling peaches, papaya chunks or pineapple chunks
3/4 cups low-fat plain yogurt or low-fat cottage cheese

Directions
Place the yogurt or cottage cheese in a small bowl. Top with your favorite fruit chunks and sprinkle with wheat germ.
Enjoy!

Kicked-Up Quesadilla

Ready in just five minutes, these healthy quesadillas obtain a bright, fresh kick from the tangy Granny Smith apple slices.

Ingredients
1/2 cup grated sharp cheddar
2 flour tortillas (whole or regular-wheat)
several thin slices of a Granny Smith apple

Directions
Evenly sprinkle a layer of cheddar cheese over one tortilla.
Arrange the apple slices on the cheese layer and cover with the remaining tortilla.
Microwave the tortillas until the cheese melts, for about ½ minutes.
Cut the tortillas into six to eight wedges. Enjoy!

Wheat Waffles

Serves 8-10

Ingredients
2 eggs
4 tbsp. oil
3 cups milk
1 tbsp. sugar
1 cup quick-cooking oats
1½ cup wheat flour
1 cup flour

Directions
While mixing the batter, heat the waffle iron.
In a large mixing bowl, combine all the ingredients. Mix until well combined.
With the help of an adult, open the waffle iron and fill its bottom with batter. Close to allow the waffle to cook.
When the waffle iron is done, carefully remove the lid. Using a fork, carefully get the waffle out of the iron or ask the adult to do it for you.
Continue making the waffles until the batter is finished.
Top with toppings that you like and serve.

Morning Milkshake
Ingredients
1 banana, frozen
1 tbsp. peanut butter
1 tablespoon honey or sugar
1/4 tsp. cinnamon
1 cup milk

Directions
Blend all the ingredients until smooth.
You may want to use fresh bananas with a handful of ice cubes if you lack the frozen bananas.

Breakfast Crostini

Ricotta is not just for lasagna —many Italian families enjoy breakfasts of fresh broad, ricotta cheese or butter and fruit preserves. It's milder than cream cheese and drier than cottage cheese, making it great for sensitive child palates.

Ingredients
1 cup strawberries, sliced
1/2 cup ricotta
1/4 of a baguette, sliced in half lengthwise
1 Tbsp. honey

Directions
Mix honey with ricotta.
Spread the honey mixture evenly over the baguette slices.
Top with strawberry slices.
You can use low-fat cream cheese in place of ricotta, if desired.

Egg Tortilla Wrap

Any leftover veggies can be used in preparation of this treat.

Ingredients
1 flour tortilla
Diced tomato and avocado
1 tbsp. shredded cheese
1 egg, cooked any way you like it

Directions
Place the cheese, tomato, avocado, and egg into the tortilla. Wrap the same way you would do to a burrito. Serve immediately with fresh salsa if you desire.

NO BAKE LIGHT MEAL RECIPES
Wonderful, creative light meal recipes for young chefs! Some recipes in this collection require adult supervision, but generally they're simple! This collection of light meal recipes will awaken the kids' creativity in the kitchen. Have fun and enjoy!

Cheesy chicken and veggie noodles

This kid-friendly noodle dish is simple for the kids themselves to make –it's full of cheese and yummy veggies!

Serving: 2
Prep time: 5 minutes
Cooking time: 5 minutes
Total time: 10 minutes
Ingredients
2 tbsp. cheddar, coarsely grated
1/2 Cup mixed vegetables, cooked
1 pkg Ramen Chicken Noodles, cooked
1/2 Cup water

Directions
Place vegetables and Ramen noodles to a microwave safe bowl.
Add water, heat slightly for 30 seconds.
Add half of the cheddar and half of the flavor sachet from the packet of the noodles to the noodle mixture; stir to mix well.
Divide the meal among the serving plates, top with the remaining cheddar and serve.

Veggie Pita

Ingredients
2 pieces of pita bread
3 Tablespoons ranch dressing or other salad dressing of your choice
1 small cucumber, sliced thin
1 carrot, sliced thin
other vegetables of your choice such as tomato slices, lettuce, etc. sliced thin
deli meat sliced thin, optional

Directions
Open your pita bread pockets and spread dressing on both sides of bread. Add sliced cucumber, carrots, or other vegetables you'd like. *You can microwave pita bread for 5-10 seconds to make them easier to open and softer.

Grapefruit Salad

Ingredients

1 medium pink grapefruit, cut into segments
1 medium orange, cut into segments
1 medium pear, sliced
1/4 Cup olive oil
1/4 Cup orange juice
2 Tablespoons rice wine vinegar
1 Tablespoon honey
chopped romaine or iceberg lettuce

Directions
Mix the cut fruit into a serving bowl. In separate bowl or quart jar blend together oil, orange juice and vinegar. Add the honey to mixture and whisk until all the ingredients are combined well.
Pour the dressing over the salad and toss to coat just before serving. Serve fruit on top of lettuce.

Creamy Grape Salad

Ingredients
8 oz. pkg cream cheese
1 Cup sour cream
2 teaspoons vanilla extract
4 lbs. seedless purple grapes or 2 lbs. purple and 2 lbs. green or red grapes
3 Tablespoons brown sugar
3 Tablespoons pecans, chopped

Directions
Kids can wash grapes and place in a serving bowl. (Our grapes were rather large so we cut them in half, kids can do this with a table knife or adult can do it.) In a mixing bowl, kids can add cream cheese, sour cream, and vanilla. Blend together. Stir into grapes and mix well.
Chill in fridge until ready to serve. Before serving, mix together brown sugar and pecans. Stir into grapes.

Eat-the-Bowl Dip
Ingredients
Carrot sticks or tortilla chips
Shredded cheese
Can refried beans
1 Green bell pepper

Directions
Place pre-cut bell pepper half on plate.
Scoop equal amounts of beans and salsa into microwave-safe bowl and mix well.
Heat bean mixture in microwave until warm but not hot, about 20 seconds. Remove with potholders.
Spoon the bean mixture into bell pepper "bowl" and top with shredded cheese.
Enjoy with tortilla chips.

Soft Chicken Tacos

Using a rotisserie chicken from the grocery store makes this an easy no bake recipe for kids.

Servings: 4

Ingredients

1/2 head green cabbage or romaine lettuce, thinly sliced
12 white corn or flour tortillas
rotisserie chicken, shredded
Low-fat sour cream (optional)
1/4 cup shredded reduced-fat Monterey Jack cheese
sliced avocado
tomato slices

Directions

Heat the tortillas in the microwave for 14-20 seconds. Place spoonful of chicken on the tortillas. Top each tortilla with 1 tsp. cheese and 2 tbsp. cabbage. If desired, add sliced avocado and tomatoes. Serve immediately with sour cream if you like.

Easy Arugula Salad

So easy for kids to prepare! It takes only minutes and looks very presentable for guests.

Total time: 15 Minutes
Recipe makes 4 servings
Ingredients
2 tbsp. olive oil or grape seed oil
1/4 cup pine nuts
1 cup cherry tomatoes, halved
4 cups fresh arugula leaves, washed and dried
1 tbsp. rice vinegar
1 large avocado, peeled, pitted, and sliced
1/4 cup grated Parmesan cheese
Freshly ground black pepper

Directions
In a large plastic bowl, combine Parmesan cheese, vinegar, oil, pine nuts, cherry tomatoes, and arugula. Season with salt and pepper, cover and shake gently to mix.
Divide the salad onto the serving plates, top with avocado slices and serve!
~Try mixed greens instead of arugula if you'd like.

Kid Friendly Pasta Salad

Prepare pasta ahead of time and store in fridge. When kids are ready for making their own lunch or dinner it will be ready. I've prepared pasta ahead of time at home for a cooking class and brought the cooked pasta in a plastic container for the kids to prepare a salad.

Total Time: 35 Minutes
Serving: 8
Ingredients
8 slices thin bacon
12 ounces fun-shaped pasta, cooked ahead of time
1/2 cup whole milk
1/2 cup mayonnaise
4 tbsp. white vinegar
24 whole basil leaves, chopped
3 green onions, thinly sliced
1/2-pound Cheddar, cubed
10 ounces grape tomatoes (red and yellow), cut into halves lengthwise
1/2 teaspoon salt
Ground black pepper
Dash sugar, optional

Directions
Cut bacon into small pieces (about ½-inch) and place them on a microwave safe paper -towel-lined plate. Cook several minutes until crisp.
In small bowl, combine vinegar, milk, mayonnaise, salt, and sugar to make the dressing.
In a large mixing bowl, stir together the bacon pieces, tomatoes, dressing, pasta, cheddar cheese and green onions. Taste for seasoning, adding more salt and pepper if desired. Finish by stirring in basil and serve.

Quick Tuna Patties

This dish gets a big tick from us - it's kid-friendly, great value and on the table in just a few minutes.

Serving: 4
Prep Time: 15 Minutes
Cooking Time: 15 minutes
Total Time: 30 Minutes

Ingredients

1/2 cup breadcrumbs, dried
2 eggs, lightly beaten
3 green onions, trimmed, finely chopped
1/8 cup vegetable oil
1 can tuna in water, drained, flaked
1 packet jasmine microwave rice
1/3 cup whole-egg mayonnaise
1 tbsp. sweet chili sauce
salad leaves

Directions

Follow the packet directions to cook rice in the microwave
Place the cooked rice on a bowl to cool slightly.
Add tuna, eggs, and onions; mix to combine well.
Divide the tuna mixture into eight portions. Roll the mixture in your hands to make balls and flatten them slightly.
Put the bread crumbs into a bowl.
Add patties and turn to coat well.
In a small bowl, combine sweet chili sauce and mayonnaise.
Serve the patties with the sweet chili sauce mixture and salad leaves.

Simple Vegetable Sushi Rolls

Sometimes called nori or maki rolls, these bite-size packets require little technology and kids can easily master how to make them. Small bamboo mats called makisu are required to make these rolls –the mats can be found in any Asian market or well-stocked supermarkets.

Use this recipe as a good opportunity to teach kids how to cut raw vegetables and make rice.

Ingredients
1 bag carrot sticks or mini-carrots
1 bunch asparagus
1 pkg. nori sheets, roasted or cooked
3 tbsp. sushi vinegar
3 cups water
3 cups sushi rice, cooked
Wasabi paste (optional)

Directions Sushi Rolls
Let the kids measure 2 cups of sushi rice into a bowl. Rinse the wash about three times by stirring in cold water and pouring off the cloudy water.
Set in a colander to drain.
Meanwhile, start preparing little piles or stations for sushi assembly.
Put water in a bowl to moist your hands while spreading the sushi rice.
If using wasabi, place a few spoonfuls in a nearby bowl and cover, for easy access, (remember to warn the kids how spicy it is!)
Half the nori sheets and store in a zipper bag to keep moist.

Vegetable Slivers Directions

Let older kids help with slicing if you're comfortable with them handling sharp knives.

This recipe only contains asparagus and carrots, but you may want a wide variety of vegetables.

Cut the carrots thinly to get translucent pieces.

Cut asparagus only once to make same length as the nori sheets.

Slightly steam the asparagus, for not more than 2 minutes.

Add vegetables to the top of your nori sheet with rice. Roll up and slice.

Microwave Baked Potatoes

This simple recipe for kids makes a great after school snack; the potatoes are very filling and economical. Sprinkle with cheese or use whatever you have in your kitchen to make a delicious topping and enjoy!

Total time: 17 Minutes
1 large potato, scrubbed clean
Your favorite toppings such as:
Garlic and parmesan
Salsa
spaghetti sauce and cheese
Baked beans and butter
Sour cream and chives
chopped ham and cheese

Directions
Using a large fork, prick all over surface of the potato. Place the pricked potato on a microwave safe dish and microwave on high for about 5 minutes.
Turn over the potato and continue microwaving for another 5 minutes.
With a hot pad, remove from the microwave and let stand for 5 minutes.
Cut crosswise on the potato face and squeeze the bottom upwards.
Add your favorite toppings and enjoy!

Ham and Pickle Rollups

Ingredients
12 Tablespoons cheese spread with bacon
8 slices of deli roast beef, chicken, or ham
24 baby sweet pickles, drained well

Directions
Spread cheese over slices of deli meat. Add pickles on the top of the cheese. Roll up and eat.

Tortilla Sandwich Rolls

An easy spin on sandwiches make this recipe for kids fun to make and eat. Opt for spinach or whole wheat tortillas for an added touch of nutrition!

Ingredients
Sandwich ingredients such as banana slices, jelly, peanut butter, cheese and turkey and mayo.
Tortilla rounds

Directions
Put the tortilla on a large plate and evenly spread over the ingredients.
Roll up the tortilla into a tube.
Slice the rolled-up tortillas into bite-sized circles and dig them into healthy snack you can easily eat with your fingers!

Egg Salad Celery Bites Recipe

Serving: 6
Total time: 5 minutes

Ingredients
4 eggs, hard-boiled
4 stalks celery cut into 1 to 3-inch pieces
1 tbsp. dill relish
3 tbsp. mayo
1 tbsp. spicy brown mustard or plain yellow mustard

Directions
Combine mustard, mayo, and relish in a large bowl.
Pour the mayo mixture the hard-boiled eggs.
Cut the eggs into small cubes with a pastry blender and stir to combine well.
Spoon the egg mixture onto celery pieces and serve.

NO BAKE SNACK RECIPES

Slam Dunk Fruit

Ingredients
16 oz., vanilla yogurt
Soft fruit such as canned pears, peaches, or berries
8 oz. cream cheese
Sliced fruit such as apples or berries for dipping

Directions
Wash and cut fruit for dipping into small slices. Set aside on a plate.
Put the soft fruit in a bowl and smash with the back of a fork or a potato masher.
Stir in the cream cheese and mix well until softened.
Add yogurt over smashed fruit mixture and stir gently.
Dip the fruit into yogurt mixture and enjoy!

Pick-Me-Up Popcorn

Popcorn and the simple shaker toppings such as parmesan cheese or cinnamon make this recipe for kids a perfect on-the-go snack!

Ingredients
Microwave popcorn
2 teaspoons of topping

Directions
Follow the package directions to the popcorn in the microwave.
When cooked, carefully open the package to avoid being burned by steam. Add parmesan cheese or cinnamon or pre-mixed topping to package and fold to close.
Shake the closed bag to coat the popcorn for a great after-school treat!

Cinnamon-chocolate seasoning: **Combine 4 tsp.** ground cinnamon and small package instant chocolate pudding and store in a container with a lid at room temperature.

Parmesan-ranch seasoning: **Combine 1 envelope** ranch salad dressing mix with ¼ cup grated parmesan cheese and store in a container with a lid in the refrigerator.

Banana Wands

For any kid, eating snacks on a stick automatically qualifies as fun! This is an easy recipe that kids will make for themselves. For a hot afternoon, kids should be encouraged to pre-freeze the bananas on the stick before coating to enjoy a cool treat.

Ingredients
Half a banana
Chocolate chips or peanut butter
1 Chopstick
Granola, crushed nuts, or topping of choice

Directions
Place chocolate chips or peanut butter into a microwave-safe bowl and heat for about 20 seconds.
Use potholders to remove the bowl from heat.
Peel the banana and slice it in half.
Place the stick into the cut end of the banana to make a handle.
Spoon chocolate or peanut butter over the banana, top with nuts, granola, or any other toppings and enjoy.

Peanut Butter-Banana Spirals

Peanut butter stars with yogurt, banana, and, for crunch, wheat germ.

Servings: 6

Ingredients
2 tablespoon honey-crunch wheat germ
2 ripe bananas, sliced
1 tablespoon orange juice
1/3 cup vanilla low-fat yogurt
1/2 cup reduced-fat peanut butter
1/4 teaspoon ground cinnamon
4 fat-free flour tortillas

Directions
In a small bowl, combine yogurt and peanut butter, stirring until smooth.
Drizzle bananas with the orange juice and toss to coat.
Spread about three tablespoon of yogurt mixture over every tortilla. Place about 1/3 cup slices of banana in one layer over each tortilla. Mix cinnamon and wheat germ and sprinkle evenly over the banana slices.
Roll up each tortilla before slicing each into 6 pieces.

Cinnamon Toast
Ingredients
2 pieces bread
1 tbsp. cinnamon
1 tbsp. butter
1 cup sugar

Directions
In a small bowl, combine cinnamon and sugar. Set aside.
Put the two pieces of bread in a toaster and toast.
Take the bread out once it pops out of the toaster and place it on the place.
Spread a thin layer of butter over the toast using the butter knife.
Sprinkle the sugar-cinnamon mixture over the buttered toast and you're done!
You may want to preserve the sugar-cinnamon mixture for the next use.

Sunshine Juice
Serving: 6
Ingredients
1 tsp. vanilla
1 cup water
1 cup milk
1 cup ice
1/4 cup sugar
1/2 cup frozen orange juice concentrated

Directions
In a blender, combine orange juice, vanilla, water, sugar, milk, and ice.
Blend the ingredients on low until the ice is chopped up, for one minute.
Pour the juice into servings cups and enjoy!

Raspberry Cream Cheese Spread
Servings: 4
Ingredients
2 bagels, halved, or 4 pieces of toast
2 tbsp. powdered sugar
3 tbsp. raspberry jam
4 ounces cream cheese

Directions
In a small bowl, combine powdered sugar, raspberry jam, and cream cheese; mix until creamy.
Serve on toast or bagels.

Cantaloupe Melon and Berry Smoothie

This is a perfect recipe when cantaloupe is in season. You may want to try it with other types of berries instead of raspberries!

Ready in 5 minutes
Servings: 2
Ingredients
1/4 Cup raspberries, about a handful
1/2 Cup low fat plain yogurt
1/2 cantaloupe, peeled, seeded, and cubed
3 tbsp. brown sugar (optional)

Directions
Combine raspberries, yogurt, sugar, and cantaloupe in a blender.
Blend the ingredients on low until smooth.
Pour into serving glasses and enjoy!

Fruity Fun Bars

Tired of waiting for the ice cream truck? Make these easy and fun frozen yogurt treats yourself! With only four ingredients and a few steps, this novelty-inspired dessert is easy for kids to make.

Prep Time: 15 min
Total Time: 8-hour 15 min
Serving: 8
Ingredients
1 can sweetened condensed milk
1 cup Trix cereal or other type
2 containers strawberry yogurt
2 containers Key lime pie yogurt

Directions
Line a medium loaf pan with foil, allowing foil edges to hang over sides of the pan. Divide milk equally between two bowls.
Stir strawberry yogurt into one bowl and lime pie yogurt into the remaining bowl.
Spread lime pie mixture into the lined pan, sprinkle with cereal.
Spoon and spread strawberry mixture on top of cereal.
Place in the freezer for at least 8 hours until firm.
Lift the frozen loaf from the pan using a foil; remove the foil and let stand for about 10 minutes. Slice up the loaf into eight pieces.

~Substitute whichever flavor yogurt you'd like.

No-Bake Cinnamon Rolls

Servings: 4

Ingredients

1/8 tsp. water
2 tbsp. powdered sugar
2 tbsp. cinnamon sugar
2 tbsp. butter
2 slices white bread, without crust

Directions

Roll the slices of the bread until very flat.
Spread butter on the bread and sprinkle with cinnamon sugar.
Start on one side and roll up each slice of the bread until tight.
Cut the rolls into about one-inch pieces.
In a small bowl, combine water and confectioners' sugar to make a thin frosting.
Drizzle the sugar frosting over the bread pieces and serve.

NO BAKE DESSERT RECIPES

With the tempting no-bake desserts like frozen fruit bites, crispy creamy ice cream squares, peanut butter pie, and cookie dough bites, who needs an oven? Check out these amazing no-bake dessert recipes for an easy treat!

Frozen Fruit Bites

A snap to assemble, these kid-friendly treats bring together sweet fruit and a refreshingly sour cheesecake-like filling.

This recipe makes enough bites for 12 kids.

Ingredients

1 tsp. lemon juice
1/2 cup cream cheese, softened
1/2 cup vanilla yogurt
12 vanilla wafer cookies
1 tsp. honey
Sliced strawberries, kiwi, or whole blueberries

Directions

Line a mini-cupcake pan with liners. Place a wafer cookie, flat side up, on each well's bottom.

Whisk together honey, lemon juice, cream cheese, and yogurt in a medium bowl until smooth. Using a spoon, scoop one heaping on top of each wafer cookie, and top each with the fruit.

Using a plastic wrap, cover the pan and place it in the freezer for about 1 ½ hours, or until the fruit bites are firm; remove, wait for about 25 minutes, and serve.

Oatmeal No Bake Cookies
Ingredients
1/4 cup peanut butter
1 cup coconut
5 tbsp. cocoa
1 tsp. vanilla
3 1/2 cups quick-cook oats
1/2 cup milk
1/2 Cup margarine or butter
2 Cups sugar

Directions
In a saucepan, combine milk, butter, sugar, and cocoa and bring to boil for 1 minute.
Stir in the remaining ingredients.
Spoon the mixture on a wax paper and chill. Enjoy!

No Bake Butterscotch Oatmeal Cookies
Ingredients
1 bag butterscotch pudding mix
3/4 cup butter
1/2 can evaporated milk
2 cups white sugar
3 1/2 cups oats, quick-cooking

Directions
Combine evaporated milk, butter and sugar in a microwaveable bowl and cook on high for about 5 minutes, stirring occasionally until the mixture boils.
Remove from the heat.
Stir in oatmeal and pudding mix.
Spoon the mixture onto lined cookie sheets.
Let sit until firm, for about 15 minutes.
Enjoy!

No Bake Peanut Butter Cookies
Ingredients
1 tsp. vanilla
3 cups oatmeal
1/2 cup peanut butter
1/2 cup milk
2 cups sugar

Directions
In a large pan, combine vanilla, milk, peanut butter, and sugar and bring to a boil.
Remove from heat and stir in oatmeal. Spoon the mixture onto a cookie sheet to cool before serving.

Lemon No Bake Cheesecake
Ingredients
Graham cracker pie crust
2 Cups whipped topping
8 oz. Cream cheese, softened
1/2 Cup boiling water
Lemon gelatin 4 serving size

Directions
Place gelatin in boiling water to dissolve.
Beat cream cheese in a separate bowl until smooth.
Gradually add in gelatin and beat to mix well.
Fold whipped topping into the gelatin mixture.
Spoon the mixture into the crust and let chill for four hours.
Serve with pie filling or berries.

Chocolate Chow Mein Noodle Cookies
Ingredients
6 oz. semisweet chocolate chips
2 Tbsp. butter
2 Cups chow mein noodles
1/2 Cup milk
3/4 Cup sugar
2 Cups mini marshmallows

Directions
Place marshmallows and mein noodles in large bowl and set aside.
Mix butter, milk and sugar in a saucepan and bring to boil.
Remove from heat and add the chocolate chips.
Stir to melt the chocolate chips.
Let stand for about 15 minutes before pouring over the noodle mixture.
Stir the mixture to coat well.
Place the mixture onto a cookie sheet coated with butter.
Refrigerate and serve.

No Bake Chocolate Almond Coconut Bites

Ingredients
1 bag semisweet chocolate morsels, melted
1 bag coconut, shredded
1 cup almonds, chopped
1 1/2 teaspoon almond extract
1 cup sweetened condensed milk

Directions
Combine coconut, almond extract, and milk in a mixing bowl.
Roll into small balls using your hands and place them on the baking sheet.
Let chill for 60 minutes.
Dip the balls into melted chocolate and return on the baking sheet to set.

Chocolate-Dipped Strawberries

Last minute is no big deal with these chocolate-dipped strawberries! They are pretty, easy to make and very appetizing.

Prep Time: 20 Minutes
Cooking Time: 5 Minutes
Ingredients
½ lb. semi-sweet chopped chocolate
20 strawberries, clean, dry with top intact

Directions
Place the in a microwave safe bowl, melt in the microwave at 30 second intervals stir until the chocolate is melted.
Line a tray or a cookie sheet with parchment paper or waxed paper.
Dip the strawberries, one after another, into the chocolate. Set the chocolate-coated strawberries on the lined paper and let cool for about 20 minutes.

Mini Pumpkin Tarts
Makes 45 tarts
Ingredients
1 (3.4-ounce) package cheesecake-flavor instant pudding and pie filling
1 tsp. pumpkin pie spice, plus extra for garnish
2 cups frozen whipped topping, thawed, plus extra for garnish
1 (15-ounce) can pumpkin
45 mini pastry shells, frozen
Mint leaves (for garnish)

Directions
Let the frozen shells thaw at room temperature for about 20 minutes.
In the meantime, mix the pumpkin pie spice, whipped topping, and pumpkin in a bowl, whisking until smooth.
Remove the shells from the freezer.
Allow them to thaw for about 15 minutes at room temperature.
In the meantime, mix pumpkin pie spice, whipped topping, and the pumpkin in a medium bowl, beating until smooth.
Add the pudding mixture to the bowl and continue whisking until smooth and thick.
Spoon about 1 tbsp. of the content into every shell, top the tarts with shipped topping, sprinkle with pumpkin pie spice and garnish with a mint leaf, if desired.

Easy Strawberry Mousse

This mouse is creamy delicious and quick to fix, and every family member will like it.

Prep Time: 10 minutes
Cook Time: 2 hours
Servings: 6
Ingredients
2 cups heavy cream
1/4 cup sugar
1/2 cup boiling water
1 (1.4 ounces) strawberry gelatin
1-quart fresh strawberries
Whipped cream and whole strawberries for garnish

Directions
Rinse and hull the strawberries before cutting each in half. Place in the food processor or blender and puree until smooth. Set aside.
Combine sugar and gelatin in a bowl. Pour boiling water over the mixture and stir until dissolved.
Pour the strawberry juice into the sugar mixture and stir to combine. If the mixture is not at room temperature at this point, refrigerate to cool.
Whip the heavy cream until stiff and fold into strawberry-gelatin mixture until blended.
Keep in the bowl or spoon into serving dishes, refrigerate for at least several hours or until set.

Chocolate Peanut Butter Bars

Chocolate and peanut butter is a favorite combination across the world and tucked into a delicious little no-bake bar makes it all the yummier!

Prep Time: 10 minutes
Cook Time: 40 minutes
Makes 30 bars
Ingredients
1 cup chocolate chips
1 cup powdered sugar
1 cup graham cracker crumbs
3/4 cup peanut butter
6 tbsp. butter

Directions
Melt together butter and peanut butter and blend well until smooth.
Add powdered sugar and cracker crumbs, combine well, and press evenly into a pan that has been lined with waxed paper or parchment pepper.
Melt the chocolate chips, stirring, until smooth before pouring over the butter mixture. Smoothen the top and place in the refrigerator for 30 minutes, until firm. Let the mixture rest for about ten minutes at room temperature.
Cut into bars and enjoy!

Surprise Pie

This recipe is simple and lots of fun for kids to make in the kitchen.

Ingredients

Fat free or low-fat chocolate pudding
Whipped cream
1 jar peanut butter
2-3 Cups Rice Krispies cereal

Directions

Place some rice krispies into a medium bowl, add some peanut butter and mix until well blended. Place the mixture into an empty crust pan and push it firmly to the pan.

Sprinkle the whipped cream on top of the Rice Krispies mixture.

Prepare the pudding and add on top of the whipped cream.

Leave in the refrigerator for half an hour before serving.

Easy Fudge Recipe

This fudge recipe is quick and easy. You can't keep enough of it around!

Ingredients
1 can sweetened condensed milk
1 stick butter
3 C. flavored chips (chocolate, butterscotch, or white chocolate)

Directions
Place all the ingredients in a microwave bowl and microwave for about 4 minutes, stirring until all ingredients are melted.
Grease a 9x9-inch pan with cooking spray. Add other ingredients such as coconut, raisins, or any other nuts if desired. Leave in the refrigerator for about four hours to set.
Cut into squares and serve immediately!

Honey Milk Balls
Ingredients
1 Cup rolled oats
1 Cup powdered milk
1/2 Cup honey
1/2 Cup peanut butter

Directions
Mix all the ingredients together, roll into small balls, and refrigerate for about 60 minutes.
You can eat the balls plain, dipped in chocolate or rolled in powdered sugar.

Printed in Great Britain
by Amazon